GRACE
AND
Tranquility

Praise for Eric Alan's
Wild Grace: Nature as a Spiritual Path

"His worthwhile voice forms a useful and needed
bridge to the truly natural language we all share and
have forgotten how to speak."
—*Publishers Weekly*

"What Hemingway would call a 'movable feast'...
Alan's astoundingly beautiful nature photography
and lyrical prose pulls the reader into a deep
contemplation of the natural world and one's
relationship to it... Few will be able to read it
without deep introspection, learning and pleasure."
—U.S. Congressman Les AuCoin (D-OR, retired)

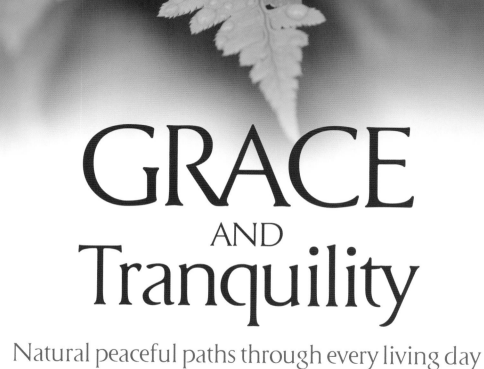

GRACE
AND
Tranquility

Natural peaceful paths through every living day

photographs and words by
Eric Alan

WHITE CLOUD PRESS
ASHLAND, OREGON

DEDICATION

To the source inside
And behind it all

And to every living element
Through which it passes

Which is to say,
To you.

Endless gratitude to:

My father, James Froyd, for making *Grace and Tranquility* possible in passing.
My mother, Shirley Froyd, for kindness and generosity beyond measure.
My sisters Karen and Carol and all my other family, in all forms. To Bev, for
a loving partnership of true grace and tranquility. To Jane, for twelve loving
years—family then and always. To all who have given friendship and support
along the path, especially everyone involved in this project: all at White Cloud
Press, Cilette & Roman of Gypsy Soul, my editor Raina Hassan, graphic designer
David Ruppe, and an endless list of others who have made it all possible.
I could never list enough names on this brief page.

Inquiries should be addressed to:
White Cloud Press, P.O. Box 3400, Ashland, Oregon 97520

Design and layout by David Ruppe, Impact Publications, Medford, Oregon

First Printing: 2010
Printed in Korea

Library of Congress Cataloging-in-Publication Data

Alan, Eric.
  Grace and tranquility : natural peaceful paths through every living day / photography and words by Eric Alan.
    p. cm.
  ISBN 978-0-9745245-8-0 (pbk.)
  1. Nature--Religious aspects. 2. Spiritual life. 3. Self-help techniques. I. Title.
  BL435.A428 2010
  202'.12--dc22
                          2010007316

"Peace is every step"
Thich Nhat Hanh

"You cannot
perceive beauty
but with a
serene mind."
Henry David Thoreau

TABLE OF CONTENTS:

A Few Tranquil Steps

Awakening

In awakening to this day, I open my eyes as if for the first time.

In awakening to you, I see that **together we are a mystery and a miracle, still half-formed and struggling to grow free.**

In awakening more, I see we are all children of stone. We are children of the soft earth, too, of moss and lichen and the smallest drops of water that feed us all. From these graceful elements our tiny faces form, insistent and beautiful.

We push our way through the soil to come here; to open our eyes and seek to see.

And what is it we seek with our shared vision? Some form of tranquility—an intricate, delicate peace we can carry through the midst of turbulence. We seek a peace we can hold inside and yet offer to others, as soft as leaves cradled in our fragile palms. We seek a peace which is as graceful and natural as those elements around us— a peace as instinctive and wild as any grace can be. We seek the peace for which we have been born.

We can walk and seek this serenity together, no matter the conflict that surrounds and stirs within us. **You and I, we can walk these places and make them home. We can find the paths of grace and tranquility within them, just as we have found each other within the open arms of the day.** We can share the earth's abundance, and by knowing its ways well, grow abundance greater still. We can deepen our gratitude for the mystery and miracle, celebrating each moment and its reflections inside.

A Tranquil Pace

On this street we walk, a stone Buddha carries coins, leaves and lichen. There's no polish to the Buddha's stone, but still he gives us clear individual reflections. Inevitably, yours will differ from mine.

When you look at the Buddha's patient palm, do you see a soul offering to share wealth or asking to receive it? The answering reflection changes according to our own offering—for his sharing or begging is truly in you and me. Tranquility is in sharing, not begging. This Buddha simply says *give what you wish to receive.*

We might as well walk slowly as we travel. There's no hurry to give or receive. **We'll find tranquility faster if we don't rush.** We may even find it immediately, simply by slowing down.

Besides, there's nowhere else to go. Tranquility must already be here, if it's anywhere.

So let's walk at our natural, patient pace. It's in walking that we return home to each other and to ourselves. Walking is our native rate of motion. We flow with ourselves then; and if we flow with ourselves, we also flow with the natural world for which we evolved. That's why our best insights often come while walking, our calmest moments, our clearest conversations.

Resting is natural, too. So let's pause and put our feet up now and then. Stillness can be our clearest state of observation. **Grace and tranquility arise through the depths of stillness, from a place beyond thinking and speaking.** Allow it. That's all that need be done, for this moment.

A Small
Peaceful Presence

The paths of grace and tranquility we travel are small, for peace is not the massive and permanent force of which we've so often dreamed. The word "peace" is burdened with impossible conceptions.

Peace is not a political solution, nor the mere absence of war, nor an earthly state of calm that quells all conflict. Peace is as transient and fragile as we who seek it.

Often, peace is not obvious when it's present. It's so subtle that it can barely be noticed without diligent attention.

Peace is as small and quiet as beautiful insect wings on almost unnoticeable flowers. It doesn't care if it's seen—it merely goes its own way at will.

This doesn't diminish peace in the slightest, nor does it make it more difficult to find and hold. Its small-ness and stealth make it easier to find. Peace is ever-present if we keep our vision open, attuned to the tiny. With openness, peace becomes our personal tranquility.

We can find as much peace and beauty in the minuscule center of one flower as in the extensive nebula of a distant galaxy. We can feel as much wonder and reverence.

The more we realize our smallness and embrace it, the larger the peace around us, and the deeper the tranquility we're able to take in.

As we take it in, we find that peace has soft edges, just as kindness does.

Peace is as gentle as the whisper of the last spring rain, encouraging pinks and greens to emerge and blend. It does not cut as it turns to inner tranquility.

We listen to grace in this rain, and look for it in the pools of water that gather.

The pools show us that peace is not one thing. It has many subtle, woven layers.

The peace here isn't just in the water, but in the ripples on the water.

Peace is in the rocks cradling the water.

Peace is in the shadow of the trees, as much as in the trees themselves.

It's in the former tree, converted to sunken log—surely a home for underwater creatures.

Peace is in the invisible life swimming within the water and skimming above it.

As we take it in, the pool also reflects the layers of grace and our inner tranquility. It reflects friendship and family and the pause called home. It shines light on attitude, work and love. Illumination lingers in the way food tastes on our tongues. Tranquility isn't just a retreat into the mountains or our inner self. Its tiny woven layers are as present in the city as anywhere.

It's as important to look for peace to absorb in the city as in the wilderness, because that's where most of us lift our faces skyward most of the time. Looking to the heights, a celestial body we see is as likely to be a balloon as a moon, and either way it's up to us to find tranquil perspective within it. Either can draw our eye to the comforting vastness within which our tiny layers of grace and tranquility are nestled.

Serenity is too important daily to be left for our rare moments in wilderness. We need it here, now, whenever and wherever here and now are. Yet if we're patient enough in awaiting its arrival we'll discover again that it's always been here, at and within our feet.

Inside the Living Storm

I hear the earth say, peace is too important to be left just for peaceful moments.

I wonder, what does that mean?

If we walk farther, I trust that the earth will reveal the answer. Here, look at the season we're now walking through. It's exquisite; but it's also harsh if we're unprepared to brave its elements—and its elements are beyond our control. Not that we can't affect them, but **living with weather has far more to do with learning to work with its ways than with changing them.**

The inherent wisdom of the winter has reflected one truth for millennia: that the graceful embrace of hard natural elements is also what allows space for tranquility in our emotional seasons. If we allow our tranquility to be determined by outside events, it will come and go in our lives by little more than mere chance. We have no choice but to accept our hardships and seek that seasonal grace—that solid grounding serenity through it all.

To open up enough to embrace
the physical and emotional winters—to
really learn how to lean into them and lose
resistance—is an accomplished art. Once we
learn that surrender, though, **the natural
elements we most resist can turn out to be
the missing soul elements that complete and
balance our lives.** They become a path towards spiritual deepening, towards compassion for others' struggles,
towards gratitude for the small blessings of easier times.

No matter how many others have walked these paths before, we
walk them uniquely, side by side. What we feel and see has never
quite been felt and seen before, and will never be experienced by
others exactly again. This winter is ours. And what more beautiful gift
could there ever be than to help each other find our paths through it?

We do not always have to create new paths. Others before us
have carved trails, via their efforts and observations and accumulated wisdom. We can wisely draw from their uniqueness to add to
our own. We can walk down the paths that others were compelled
to create by desire or circumstance. The paths are history and
instinct passed down. The paths are communities across time,
unified though too separated by years to even speak. The paths are
the fresh snows that help us to leave clear tracks for others, even as
the same snows chill and slow us.

We will walk these winters inside the endless living storm, and
we will be the heat, the slow, steady fire that keeps each other warm.
We will not wait for the warmth to come from outside, for lasting

peace is purely internal—it's the only peace we can count on. Equanimity: to face whatever storm is given and to bring calm to it instead of adding to its turbulence—that is the graceful art of tranquility. It's an art of finesse, as intricate as the creation of a symphony. Thus peace must also be the art of accepting our own imperfections in its creation and maintenance. Peace is a place to which we endlessly return after straying or being swept away. Being at peace means coming to a stable equilibrium, so that when we're disturbed, peace is where we naturally return. Even our deepest lasting peace dances and bends, as does a candle flame.

Taking time for beauty is more important than ever when the surrounding storm is raging. To appreciate the beauty within the storm will return us to tranquility more quickly than any other path. Around all that is dead and dormant, there is always color, life and fire that will birth new living wonders from within what appears to be empty.

Who are the visionaries of the ages before us to which we still turn? They are the masters who managed to bring tranquil beauty into the troubles around them. The ones who practiced peace in times of war, brought insistent integrity into calming the illness of violence, found nobility in resistance, reached for poetry instead of weapons, forgiveness instead of vengeance. And for every iconic soul who has found a place in historic memory for choosing that tranquil path—often at great cost—there are countless ones who have chosen the same in small anonymous ways, through equally pure gestures that will never be known beyond their own neighborhoods. We must be those choosing grace and tranquility, not for glory but for service and its joys, unremembered though it may be. And the harder the small storms rage around us, the more important it is that we continue to make that choice, one small step at a time.

Tranquility is not a simple practice. And yet it is. For simplicity is a vital compositional aspect of peace. This art of walking through the world together is only complicated by the unnecessary complexities we invent.

To keep our lives and our aims simple assists us immeasurably in the growth of our tranquility. To tell the truth is far simpler than to weave webs of deceit. To need few things is a vastly easier path to true riches than is the acquisition and hoarding of material wealth. To do few things patiently and with great presence is a far deeper experience than to do many things hurriedly and on the surface. The fundamentals of home, family, sunshine, laughter—these are the natural compositional elements of tranquility that have been passed down to us. They're so nearly constant that they're almost a still life, like a vase in a window. But life is anything but still, ever-shifting even as we breathe in silence, just being with the beautiful, simple day. The mere truth of existence is simple enough and beautiful enough to bring tears.

We may need a torrent of tears to keep our grace and tranquility, and not always tears of joy. We'll cry many times as we surrender to the shifts of peace and struggle, which will newly mystify us with their ways each day. Our tears may merge with the world's tears and pool on every surface we see.

There's no point in trying to distinguish whose tears are whose. Let them all be. They're a part of tranquility, too. Our deepest grieving requires our deepest expression for cleansing.

Take refuge in this: our body only carries so much water. **Our capacity for sorrow is limited by our size and short lifetimes.**

Our current storms will cease regardless of how much we kiss or curse them. Our tears will inevitably be over.

In the end, tranquility and grace return through equilibrium and balance. **Growth will always part, simply to rejoin.** The blue of the sky will always be balanced by the harder solid browns of the soil. Summer will be tempered by winter. Aging will be tempered by birth. It's the constancy within the shifting nature of things. It's one universal path we share, and there is plenty of space and time on it for all of us, without hurry or concern. We belong here together.

Sometimes in the journey there's nothing to do but watch for an instant. **There's often so much less that needs to be done than we believe.** There's so much less weight to carry when we release the struggle of chasing off all storms. We can neither create nor prevent the rainbows that follow the storms. We can only have gratitude for the blessing of being with them.

Our true awakening begins then, as we discover within the storm that tranquility is elemental within us. The storm has grace too. We're made from it, as inherently as we're made from the soil. No storm destroys our fundamental nature.

Gathering Strength

Even one drop of water contains uncountable riches. For what is truer wealth than the water that feeds all seeds of life? Without water, no life would grow. Water allows us each to open our eyes and go on our minor journeys. Water allows the profound truth to inform those journeys.

Water allows me to speak. Water allows you to listen. Water is the basis of family, of love, of every other center of life.

Look at any average drop: it's amazing. Like any of us, it's average and essential at the same time. It can be simultaneously unnoticed and vital.

Water will sometimes find its way through tears. That's average and essential, too. **Even our most painful tears—*especially* our most painful ones—can later prove to have watered the seeds of our happiness.**

Tears can also water our gratitude for our blessings. And tears can be born of compassion, beauty or joy as easily as being born of suffering. Joyful tears are deep fonts of strength, insight, clarity. Tears can even combine our emotional extremes, blending joy and suffering as one.

We need our tears, whatever they're born of. We need every bit of strength we can gather, from every source—for tranquility doesn't come from a place of weakness or meekness. Nor does it come from a place of numbness. Our peace is in feeling all joys and pains. Our grace is there too. Daring that much feeling is not for the faint of heart, but it is natural. It is a challenge for which we were born prepared.

There is grace in the strength and beauty that grows in the odd places where we unexpectedly root. Tranquility is in knowing that we, the average, have the strength to crack streets, walls and other barriers with our insistent, small beauty. Tranquility is in knowing that small cracks are enough. We can root in the smallest ones and grow strong enough to widen them until the former barriers are completely broken. **We can gather strength simply by standing still as we grow.**

When we're in motion instead, our tranquility is in knowing that our path need not be linear. Despite our most rigid efforts to keep our courses straight, lines and their shadows bend and zigzag.

So whatever our method of travel, we must have the strength to zigzag with them. **Our best paths will curve and flow. They will be traveled according to the contours around and inside us.**

Our grace is in accepting, even embracing, that we'll have to improvise our way across and through danger, using whatever materials of earth and soul are at hand.

Tranquility is in seeing the elegance of even our roughest improvisations.

When others can't see the elegance of our mere survival, or when we can't see it ourselves, tranquility can be a lonely or distant proposition. **You might feel tranquil, but still feel as though you're the only creature for immeasurable miles who does.**

Whether alone or in great company, **grace and tranquility require standing firm with supple but fierce resoluteness.** Almost always, there are easier places to stand than places of peace.

Tranquility is naturally dependent upon survival, and it demands that we retain strength and protection, no matter how soft our hearts may be at the core. There are times when life is on the line, and tranquility with it. Life requires vigilance. **Tranquility has hard points and sharp edges.**

Tranquility has seasons, and summer can be as harsh as winter at times. Summer is a storm of heat and dryness as lethal as the cold. The apparent loneliness of tranquility can feel so empty at first. It's lonely out in this desert until we learn to see its life, well-camouflaged as it is. Emptiness turns to spaciousness when we embrace it, though. And **spaciousness turns out to contain the beauty and life of the entire world.**

Spaciousness
(the Key)

Accepting the difficult and desolate in our journey is a transforma-
tive step. It allows us to see the difficult and desolate for what they
are—forms of vibrant abundance with miraculous amounts of life
and wisdom within. With our strength gathered, we can unlock
their hard secrets.

There are infinite keys to this vision. In every moment, our key
is new; our grace and tranquility are different.

**One essential master key is this: emptiness is never
empty,** whether it's the supposed void of interstellar space or the
even more limitless expanses inside the soul's darkest night.
Embracing what seems empty is the path to finding that it always
contains more fullness than we could ever hold.

In physical space, emptiness has edges and shapes as sharp as the shapes around it. Even a vacuum has light within it, passing through. Even a dark place has matter. True emptiness has never been discovered—particularly not on earth, where atmosphere pervades all places where ground and water do not. We have never experienced pure emptiness.

In emotional space, what we call emptiness is a definite and demanding feeling. It's excruciatingly real—and far from empty. There's pain within it; and within our pain are rich, complex layers of histories, emotions, relationships, experiences and direct connections to the experiences and emotions of others. **A direct path beginning in our emptiness can eventually be traced to every soul, feeling and event that has ever existed on earth.** What could possibly be less empty than that?

Our own personal emptiness wasn't there at the moment of our conception, either. It has an individual form and contents that grow as we do. It's not even merely contained within us. We weave it around us like a web, with its connections to events, experiences and

other living beings. Our emptiness is itself a living being of experience—
a precious life worthy of examination with curiosity and awe. Looking at
our emptiness in tranquility is like examining a spider web to discover
the intricacy and beauty of its structure, instead of just cursing it when it
brushes uncomfortably against our face. As with one drop of water,
there's a whole miniature living world to be discovered within it.

Our personal emptiness may have memories of events—either
experienced or absent—inscribed within it. It may have expectations
unmet, hopes unfulfilled. It may have unkind words that froze into
place, whether words from others or (worse) from within. It may have
traumatic accidents or other more personal misfortunes; even good
fortune handled badly. Over the course of a lifetime, it will probably
have all of those in it. Yet over time, all can be woven into wisdom
and contentment, as the tears of emptiness water the seeds of
happiness and gratitude for the deep blessing of merely being alive.
**The intricate web of our emptiness becomes one of our
most beautiful creations, as we transform its sorrows.**

If you look as deeply into emptiness as fullness, you'll find connection to the exact same events, people, experiences, places. **Emptiness and fullness are inseparable twins,** just as light and shadow are, sharpness and blur, brilliant red and subdued green. Eventually, the main difference is an embrace—a compassionate, complete soul embrace that turns your wounds into gifts, your pain into wisdom, your resistance into gratitude.

To begin that embrace is to be able to face each element of your emptiness without flinching and seek within it the seed of some insight, some wisdom, some depth of living experience unavailable elsewhere. As soon as we can find that insight and demystify its elements, our emptiness begins to transform.

With diligent acceptance of what is, even tragedy can be trans-
formed over time from a killing vacuum to a rich gift of service—
though its vast price and the scars we carry as beauty marks may
always remain. It's the one who knows every inch of the hard way
who really learns what the way is. Sometimes it takes millions of
our illuminating tears to make the richness within our emptiness
visible; but **sometimes one of us can cry tears so that
thousands of others don't have to.** Those tears, then, are a
great gift of tranquility to the world.

When I was young, I couldn't see my pain as a potential gift to others. I spent too much time wishing for the transformation of my emptiness, instead of acting on the transformation. I approached change as a wishing well, passively tossing hopes in. There was no tranquility in that. There was no gathering of strength, no embrace, no gift.

To see the world as a wishing well is false. More truthful is to envision it instead as a garden, governed by principles gardeners know well. The magic of our imagination still provides a beginning, but to become successful gardeners **we must dig into the earth with daily hard work to accompany our visions.** Only then do life gardens blossom into their full potential.

Our small, persistent growth is enough to split fences and crack streets because of the spaciousness within them—because there's a place to begin. There's room to grow roots even within the hardest surface. The hardest of our troubles leave similar room to begin.

Emptiness doesn't exist; yet there's spaciousness within every solid form and transience within them all as well. **Even the most seemingly impenetrable wall before us, whether literal or figurative, inevitably will eventually be broken.**

If emptiness and solidity are both illusion, what's left along these paths? Spaciousness—and the room to find the richness of tranquility reflected within all of it. Indeed, that is the key.

Richness, the Wind

Richness is a wind we stir as we walk. Like the physical wind, it makes its clear presence known through what it moves. Richness makes its presence known in our spirits, through all the beauty it draws our eyes toward.

Wind seems to grow from nothing. A wind is no less rich for the smallness of its beginnings. A beginning is all it needs. It, too, can manifest from within what seems empty and blow through what seems solid.

Even a full-blown wind is only a trace
of a much larger, multi-dimensional wind
of which we can only sense but one aspect.
**Most of spirit can only be seen
through reflection—and it's more
beautiful, softer that way.**

It's the merger of softness and clarity
that gives eventual depth to our most calm,
centered vision.

At times this may mean we only sense the
presence of richness, without knowing quite
what the richness is. Richness can take ages to
reveal itself. We simply have to trust.

Even when the essence of richness is opaque or elusive to us, signs and symbols of its spirit may suddenly appear, if our eyes remain open to it and we trust in its existence. It may be symbolized by something as pure and stark as a dove on a roofline, or by something as indirect as a breeze caressing grasses. In any detail of our surroundings we may sense the spirit within and beyond and find our tranquility within awareness of that rich wind, which always stirs our hair as we go together, one breath and one step forward at a time.

So let us let go again—and again and again—of the illusory emptiness we've held so tightly. We don't need its illusions any longer. **Everywhere we go, we go with the wind of richness in our hair, and we go there together.** There are countless numbers of us, all seeking to find and feel what's always been here. So close your eyes with me, breathe and feel enveloped in that rich breeze blowing off the sea of spirit again.

Into the Endless Richness

There's so much beauty to embrace that our troubles can't touch. Our troubles are so small compared to beauty, though it often doesn't seem that way.

We can touch graceful levels of tranquility just by looking at that greater beauty. We can touch it more deeply by seeing ourselves within it. We become centered by beauty when we feel our place of belonging there.

Look deeply into this river, this aspect of our beauty and soul. Surely the river is already pregnant with spring; but it doesn't show yet. What shows is the full white richness of *now*, with every color not absent but simply latent. If you've ever seen cold December light scatter off snow, you'll know the vivid spectrum I mean. We are the same way, with every aspect of richness and beauty latent within us, only visible through empathy, compassion and stillness.

Seeing latent beauty is like seeing the tiny materials of life with which only microscopes can first be intimate. We have to see it once to comprehend it; but then imagination reveals it from that moment on, every time we look.

It's necessary to sense the small and subtle to really know the greater beauty of the endless richness, for **beauty is shy.** It likes to hide its purest face. And it can easily be driven away by excessive force of affection.

Beauty has no need to call attention to itself—a beautiful quality of modesty, in its own right. Beauty seems content to be partially concealed, or unnoticed. Beauty is vulnerable, and often easily wounded.

In some way that our senses are too limited to understand, I believe beauty knows it exists, and beauty knows its fragile nature, as much as all sentient creatures do. We are born within beauty, and thus are children of it; yet beauty remains constantly impressionable. Beauty grows in direct relation to our touch of it; and also in defiance of our every effort. If our touch is unskillful we may easily damage it, but beauty will still insistently return after our damaging touch is gone. Beauty is resilient.

Grace may not return in a form we would design or choose. Beauty is a free spirit, gathering strength within every glistening drop of that wild, life-giving water, best and deepest when untamed. Beauty is diminished by any form of captivity, as we are.

Beauty is wise, too, for it gives of itself rather than looking to receive. To give what we wish to receive is the essence of grace and tranquility, so to nurture tranquility, we have to create beauty—little shining drops of singular beauty.

Single beautiful drops gather into the strength of exceptional shimmering lakes, deep enough to swim in and far too large to ever swim across. **The layers of beauty around us are so deep that only a tiny fraction of them will ever be seen,** even within the one place we currently focus our eyes.

How many beautiful things we can't see, even within these small waters! So many other beautiful things behind us, which we're missing right now. And still more beautiful things you're seeing that I don't, just by your difference from me. The richness is endless just in this one small place we're standing.

Look beyond this place anyway. The alchemy of imagination and science has opened visions to us almost too beautiful to comprehend. Light that has traveled from the other side of the universe for billions of years to reach us is now arriving—and it feels like a letter from family. Other beautiful galaxies, formerly shy with us, now allow themselves to be seen. The far edge of the universe permits us to be intimate with it for the first time. We can sense the immense beauty of our home with a clarity none before us have known.

But in these modern urban days, we must often look between wires to see even the moon. We need every tool of instinct and memory just to remember the existence of the stars our ancestors once steered by. **The ghostly dance of urban shadows places a veil between us and the heavens.** Beauty gets shy once again.

So how do we walk through this richness? What path do we follow, given the invisibility of many layers of beauty, and the existence of more grace than we can comprehend?

We follow the path of that next single step, which is beautiful too. It's all we need to know.

Tranquil
Abundance

The soils of earth are so abundantly rich that nearly anything can take root in them. Nearly any kind of life can find a way to sprout, crawl or soar into being. In earth's ingenious and insistent quest to be alive, its creativity appears limitless.

Earth also seems unconcerned about which forms of life succeed. Antelope or predator cheetah, human being or deadly microbe, rose or poison oak—the earth seems to pass no judgment. If a life form succeeds within the context of the greater being, it's welcome. That is equality of the most primal kind.

The wild potential of life's abundance is miraculous and beautiful. Its indifference to form also lends itself to being bent. **Our power to guide abundance makes it imperative that we take great care with what we plant and tend.** It isn't just gardens of food and flowers we tend, either. Our souls are as fertile as the soil; our emotions and actions similarly root. Emotional and spiritual life forms thrive if we nourish them, whether they are intentional or accidental, positive or negative. Abundance will support them without prejudice. Our life brings life to our inanimate creations too: we grow cars more abundantly than roses; our computers host viruses as virulent as biological ones. Our buildings can be beautiful—and still imprison us, even as they reflect the cleverness we often cultivate more keenly than wisdom.

It's vital that we always ask ourselves: what growth are we tending with these steps we're taking, this conversation we're having?

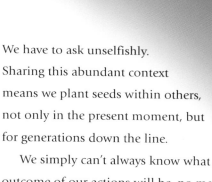

We have to ask unselfishly.
Sharing this abundant context
means we plant seeds within others,
not only in the present moment, but
for generations down the line.

We simply can't always know what the outcome of our actions will be, no matter how conscientiously we seek to move with grace and wisdom. When intentions go awry or when we cannot predict our effects, we have to forgive ourselves for our limits. In the end, tranquility means contentment with knowing only a small bit of our effects.

Our limits are not a shortcoming. It's enough to know how to plant and tend seeds. We don't have to know how a seed becomes a brilliant flower, as long as the seed knows. We just have to trust sometimes: trust ourselves, trust the earth, trust that **abundance doesn't always require us to create or manage it.**

We also have to release the narrow notion that abundance is something merely measured in money. Not all circles of richness are coins. What greater abundance could there be than the circles in this garden of vibrant hues, free for us to walk in at whatever pace we choose?

Nothing is more at the heart of abundance than the rush of a full river. A river is an endless collection of those vital single drops, gathering strength together like we do as individuals, each giving life and receiving tranquility.

When we see the rivers rushing in the winters, we can already see the greens of spring exuber-
antly bursting forth, if we're observant. When we feel their deep sound as a vibration in our mar-
row, we can sense the rivers of our own veins pulsing in time to the rivers' rhythms. Our
aliveness is refreshed.

Summer then brings an abundance of lightness and light. We can bask in it, absorbing it
until it becomes a part of our core. Then autumn will bring an abundance of color again,
and an abundance of letting go. Winter will bring its abundant rivers, rains willing;
the dark will bring inward time to explore the wealth of our souls. Then spring
will bring its exuberance and new growth again. **All physical and
emotional seasons contain unique forms of abundance.**
And no matter the season, look at the spacious abundance
of sky above us! It's a constant abundance that
far transcends us.

Spaciousness is a precious form of abundance, regardless of what's within it. To be alone (or together) in wide open spaces is less frequent now than it was on a less crowded planet, but there are still shorelines to be walked that will get us in touch with that feeling—not to mention endless cornfields, forgotten mountain trails, and other unnamed places of refuge.

Even in the city, stretches of openness still open up when we're watchful. Openness reaffirms itself unexpectedly, at odd times and places.

Spaciousness and abundance inside: that's our ultimate goal. **Once we establish a viable inner habitat for optimism, happiness, abundance, grace and tranquility, they begin to thrive of their own accord,** until we're nearly overcome by the bright colors of their growth.

Memory of this growth becomes our most enduring abundance as we age. The days that are good now will always have been good later. Within us, they become untouchable.

That untouchable peace of abundance is priceless. So come now, let's walk other paths of tranquility together and better learn how to tend to the tender and green.

A Gardener's Tranquility

Those who garden know the magic and mystery of bringing forth growth. The grounded feeling gardening brings is evident. Gardening requires persistent work, but it doesn't have to be a struggle. It merely requires diligent attention to living detail. It demands constant, deep listening to the needs of what's growing. An unselfish satisfaction then flourishes: the gardener's tranquility.

We're always gardening with every physical and spiritual move. We might as well learn to cultivate well, so we can wake to that gardener's tranquility.

We tend not only to plants, but to words and relationships. We cultivate love, home-cooked meals, and laughter. We tend to these as a traditional gardener tends sunflowers.

If we garden well, we're cultivating another path of grace and tranquility. We're watering our seeds of happiness. On occasion we may still grow our emptiness inadvertently as well, and have to transform it later with our embrace. Regardless, we're always fertilizing our inner soil—and an abundance of memory will result, whether thorny or sweet.

As we garden, we're always reshaping beauty that already exists. We're only guides. The soil we work with was already here before us, as was all that we're made of ourselves.

What we guide into showing its shy beauty begins and ends with what (and whom) we touch. So we need to be careful with how our touch shapes all we contact: it's not only our purpose and legacy—it's who we are right now. **The beauty we shape, shapes us in return.** Distance between creator and creation vanishes.

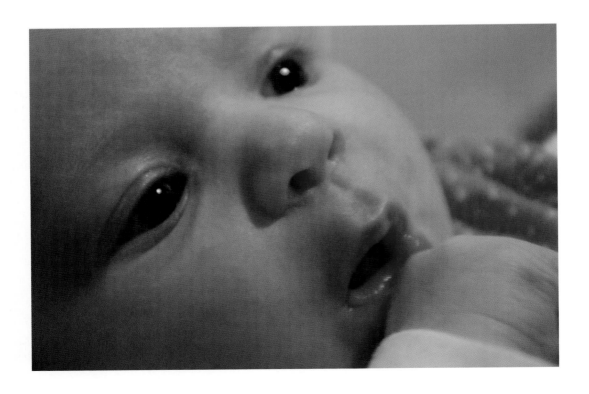

It's vital to nurture the garden's peace, but we often garden so heavily in the growth of cement, steel and other hard surfaces that greenery is almost a ghostly city memory, receding in rear view. It's no accident then that in parallel, we garden hard emotions and barriers between each other.

Softer emotions and greener leaves use their tenacity to break the hardness. We must assist and nurture them in their natural persistence. When we touch them, they touch us back with the most natural forms of tranquility. **We can't afford to miss the green beauty in this life, for which we were born. It's at the core of the grace and tranquility we seek.**

In the old schoolroom days, the classic student offering was an apple for the teacher. But in a deeper sense, the apples are the teacher. And also the lesson. And the reward of the lesson applied. The apples teach us how to grow, how to garden, how to appreciate the taste of the sweet. They teach us about ripeness, transience and the power of a seed.

Their cycles teach of
patience and timing our own
rhythms to those of the earth.
They show us the lesson of being
dependent upon roots and
branches beyond our own fruit.
    The entirety of the wild earth
needs our delicious attentiveness
and listening, for its bountiful
garden contains all core lessons.
    In every symbiotic relationship,
from daily intimacy to casual busi-
ness, we repeat the pattern of the
garden flowers, each different and yet
able to share space to bloom.
    Just keep gardening. That's what the
world says to us when the blooms of our
efforts aren't evident. Just keep gardening. We must
have compassion for the soil
and for ourselves. We will bloom when
conditions are right—even in the face
of hard walls.

**Our growth is inevitable, and
inevitably surprising.** What forms
of happiness will grow from our seeds?
Which faces of abundance will dare
smile? What spaciousness awaits discovery within our private emptiness?
What bitter challenges will balance our
joy? This garden we're in—this garden

we are—is so restless and persistent, always insisting upon some life but never the same life.

This daily gardening is meticulous and lifelong work. But **one of the key aspects of our work—not separate from the work at all—is the task of taking time just to enjoy the garden.** That sacred time is truly our harvest. It's one of the most sacred and primal things we do. It's what keeps the joy in the rest of our struggle. It keeps larger perspective within our view of small daily tasks. It allows beauty to see itself, through our beautiful eyes. It allows graceful, tranquil paths to be revealed to us, right where they've always been—right where we already are, here in the center of the great garden.

Family Letters

There are times when walking these paths feels lonely, tranquil or not. We become disconnected from our sense of family, failing to recognize its constant existence around us.

It can be hard to even know where to place our next footstep, now and then. Looking back, the path of our life becomes as clear as a sidewalk through sand. But it's difficult to trust the path's existence in front of us, even though its clarity is always glaring in retrospect, and so must have existed, just waiting to be revealed. To trust is to believe in the hidden wisdom of time. Trust pulls our one true path out of the infinite options before us at every moment.

Trust in each other keeps us walking side by side. **Trust creates family.**

Loneliness and solitude are both members of our family, related yet distinct. We can live a life of deep solitude and rarely feel loneliness. And we can feel loneliness despite being surrounded by all the love and companionship our souls could desire. Being separated from ourselves is what turns solitude to loneliness, what keeps us apart from family. It's separation from ourselves that leads us into the illusion that we're separate from others.

Centered solitude is a coming home to ourselves, and thus, to family. Tranquility is in any moment of arrival.

Ever since our primordial ancestors first crawled out of the sea to brave the experiment of land, we've been looking back across that land and out to mother sea, dreaming of someone who will magically appear to assuage our loneliness. But living as an individual always brings discomforts, including moments of feeling separate and lonely, no matter how illusory. We're all born at different moments, move along unique paths and die just as uniquely. On the surface, the nature of being is solitary.

When we recognize that there are always others on the shore with us, they become the bedrock for us, and we become the bedrock for them. **We're the family for the lonely, especially when we're lonely ourselves.** We're unified by emotions, even when no words or other perceptions cross the distances between us. Together, we're all sculpted slowly by the tide, strong and defined within it. And we're the tide as well, made from water more than anything.

When we recognize the one at our side who assists us most naturally in soothing that fundamental lonely ache, we begin to blur and merge with them more consciously. We become more aware that we're joined below the surface of the sea and sand, as bedrock is. We recognize how solid we are together, as unquestionably majestic as the sea stacks above the waves. We feel with undeniable presence how our bedrock all joins underneath the sea in ways usually unseen. There is no more tranquil feeling than that deep, calm sense of knowing. There is no stronger sense of family.

Everywhere, we can see families alongside and within ours. **From sea snails to sand ants, families of small creatures move with collective purpose, purely focused in a way to which we only aspire.** How much wisdom there is in their gathering just to eat and to be. Doing the same with our own family and

community is some of the deepest richness we can experience. That simplicity
is one of our primary longings and one
of our surest sources of tranquility.

It's wise for us to give heed to these
families and our place within them.
Our size and form may differ, but **we're
so similar to ones we barely notice, even if we find them alien or
fearful.** They have knowledge and instinct that carries its own tiny wisdom.
Their needs and desires parallel ours: to
eat, live natural lives, find a mate and create children who will
carry on. We, too, build homes and do our best to give our family
safe haven there. Our constructions and theirs have parallels. The
webs spiders weave have similarity to many of our nets and fences,
though what we wish to catch and contain may differ.

Our similarities to others may be masked at first glance, yet even in that we find reflections. Haven't we all masked ourselves at times, not wishing to be revealed? Right there is kinship with what's guarded. And the closer we look, the more we see that **even masks bear the shape of the faces they pretend to conceal,** faces that mirror our own.

Masks and cold metals may also contain warmth and wisdom below their hard surfaces. There is life under the layers and inside our symbols. What we sculpt from raw ore is reflective of the paths we choose to walk, and how we treat family. Given metal, do we sculpt weapons or a figure of the goddess of compassion?

The goddess of compassion is very closely related to you. No matter if she's masked, you have her spirit deeply, innately inside you.

Countless other gods and goddesses are with us, too. Among many, the gods of awareness and patience reside in

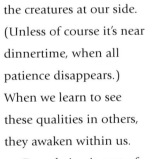

the creatures at our side. (Unless of course it's near dinnertime, when all patience disappears.) When we learn to see these qualities in others, they awaken within us.

Every being is part of our spiritual family, always beside us. Solitude and loneliness are as illusory as

emptiness. And all we have to do to know that, feel it, be it, is to breathe slowly and deeply enough to take it all in. **Breath is where this shared family life begins.**

Our family life began far before our first personal breath, though. The extensive roots of our ancestry are deep in the earth's own breaths, and spread far across the air. Family is not a narrow clan, defined by a single stream of blood passed down. Family is the ongoing mingling of different bloods. Creating family is the process of reaching out across differences to merge, and in the process creating new life—different life than has ever existed before. Making family is an action that brings down borders. Recognizing family is the ability to see that the borders are only our own mind creations.

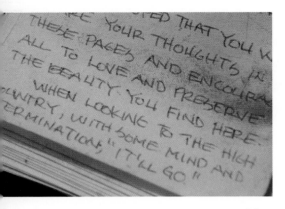

In this creation process, we can think of our footsteps as communication. Community and communication share a root, and **this next step that we are about to take is in some small way a character in a word in a sentence in a letter to family.** This next step will say something important about who we are, where we are going, how we are going there, who we are choosing to go there with and how we are treating them along the way.

We must ask ourselves: to whom in our family will we be writing with this step? Is it the insect underfoot? Is it the one we're holding hands with or conflicting with so intimately? Is it a stranger we barely notice? Is it the greater unseen that science and spirit say permeates all? Is it the wood or dirt or concrete of the path itself? Is it the galactic light? Is it the living abundance? What do our footsteps intend to say? More importantly, what do our steps actually say, when we see their tracers in the dust?

There are whole libraries and bookstores filled with letters to us from our family, just waiting to be read and embraced. At this very moment, millions or even billions of family members are also reaching out this way across miles and centuries and belief systems. All we have to do is really notice how many seek to embrace us—not only through words but through music and film and all

other forms—and we'll know how much family we've always had. There are no strangers, in the end.

Through appreciation of family and our dedication to it, we achieve a tranquility that nothing can take away. Our memories of sharing days together, especially the quiet slow days as the colors change around and within us, are grace that we will take with us when we go.

At that point our divinity becomes fully realized within us, and if divinity needs to find expression in spray paint on a tin wall on the bad side of the railroad tracks, in the company of broken glass, so be it. Divinity is universal, as present everywhere as the family we once failed to notice.

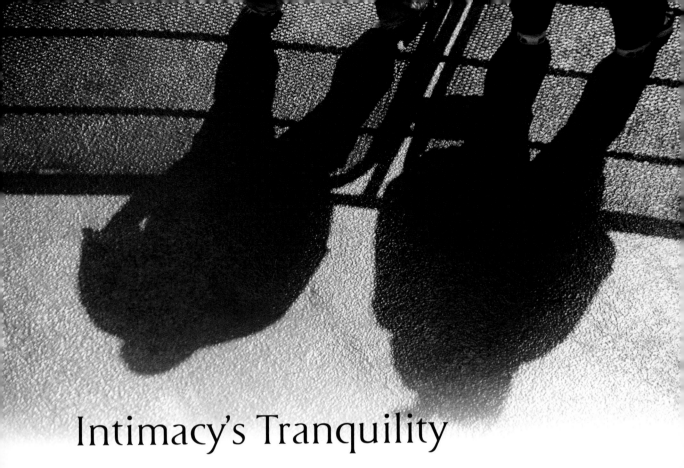

Intimacy's Tranquility

Intimacy is truth. For us to be intimate means we know each other's details and secrets clearly. It means we understand unspoken thoughts; intuitively we sense emotions. This is human beauty at its best. Yet intimacy also means we bear the brunt of each other's careless habits, by virtue of sheer proximity. We see deeply who we are—the deepest shadows we cast—and choose to stay together anyway. That's intimacy in its raw, stark form. It's a tremendous honor, never to be taken for granted.

Intimacy doesn't always grow a gardener's tranquility. Along with bringing our highest beauty to light, our intimacy reflects all of our worst aspects. It can be excruciating to be the garden as well as the gardener. What a challenging responsibility, to be the one who needs to grow!

If we can stay with intimacy and its challenges, we eventually grow security and tranquility of the highest form. Intimate love gives us the opportunity to see the divinity within our imperfections.

Intimate love reaches outward with its vision as well. In love, we may find ourselves seeing our lover's passionate essence in every tree, sweet fire flaming from our most intimate sacred spaces, as brightly as the blazes of fall. We may hear their voice in every breeze and bird song, reminders of the joy intimacy nurtures.

At times, intimacy is still an uncomfortable, painful experience. Even then—especially then—intimacy is the most purifying living force of growth in the garden.

Intimacy's tranquility is in surrendering to the purifying force of its joyful and painful truths.

To be tranquil within intimacy means surrendering to the limits of its clarity, as much as to its truths. No one else can completely see into our intimate relationships from the outside; but we can't see the wholeness of our self and love from within, either. After extended intimacy, our personal edges may become uncomfortably unclear. We can easily lose sight of who we are, except in relation to the one beside us. It's maddening enough to make loneliness seem attractive again, from a distance—for loneliness is narrower, but easier.

Given compassion, we realize the normalcy of phases of intimate confusion. They're shifts of the storm, times when our

center must move. They're times to throw our heads back and laugh at the absurdity of it all. And listen, as we laugh! Hear the echo of a million global laughs in our greater family, sharing the feeling. It's the sound of the futility of even pretending to be alone. Intimacy's tranquility is found within compassion for ourselves in intimacy's puzzle. **In the end, there's no way to avoid intimacy.** We might as well relax into it. When we do, being so closely present with each other reveals again just how sacred life is.

We often define intimacy as sexual and emotional closeness with one other person. But if we define intimacy more openly— as any true closeness—we find many different intimacies in the great garden, beginning with the true closeness we have with our offspring. With whom could we possibly be more intimate than the ones we've created?

We can also be intimate with the raw, natural land. We can be intimate with the urban city constructions that daily surround us. Our emotional intimacy with animals has a truth of its own. We can be intimate with friends and even adversaries. Music offers pathways to intimacy as well, as does art, as do all forms of creative expression. And what's more intimate than our connection to the overall greater spirit?

When we fully relax into intimacy's tranquility, it's then that we see ourselves and our infinite intimate family with full clarity. We see all of this family as the center of a cathedral. We see the

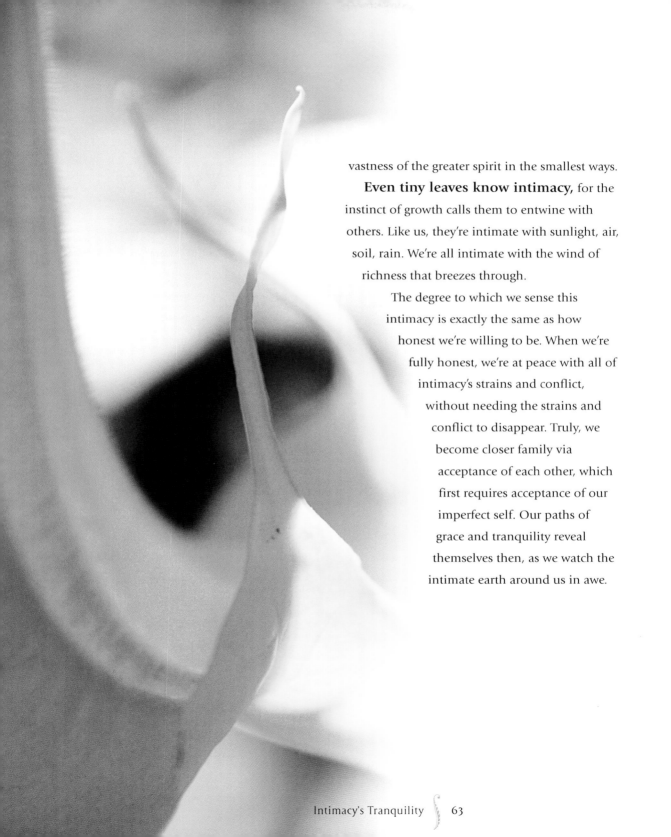

vastness of the greater spirit in the smallest ways. **Even tiny leaves know intimacy,** for the instinct of growth calls them to entwine with others. Like us, they're intimate with sunlight, air, soil, rain. We're all intimate with the wind of richness that breezes through.

The degree to which we sense this intimacy is exactly the same as how honest we're willing to be. When we're fully honest, we're at peace with all of intimacy's strains and conflict, without needing the strains and conflict to disappear. Truly, we become closer family via acceptance of each other, which first requires acceptance of our imperfect self. Our paths of grace and tranquility reveal themselves then, as we watch the intimate earth around us in awe.

Intimate with War

There is little tranquility in the midst of war. Wars are so blindly traumatic and gruesome that only the greatest masters of peace—if anyone—can maintain a semblance of equanimity in war's presence. To be intimately touched by it is to be scarred by it forever, if not destroyed.

Everywhere, there are reminders of war's long history—often looking honorable and noble. We lose slow track of the causes and casualties; and as the immediacy fades, so does the horror. **The lessons of tragedy too often die with those who suffer it.**

We can keep those lessons alive and reduce war by seeing more clearly what it is. We need to become intimate enough with war to know its true nature without it ruining us. We need to observe war without judgment so that it can change of its own evolutionary accord.

Conflict and competition are natural. That is war's essence. Conflict and competition are essential aspects of the survival-of-the-fittest system of which we're but a small competing part. War is merely our extreme, bent expression of the natural conflict dance, fueled by tools too large. As outsized and horrifying as it has become, war doesn't result from a tragic flaw in human character. It comes from a healthy instinct gardened poorly.

If you doubt that war is natural, watch children's elemental warrior games. In part they imitate observed adult violence; but instinctive battle games also teach survival skills that would've once been essential. From the beginning, many of us need to build our forts and defend them. We are compelled to conquer the neighborhood dirt piles. We fight.

Still, most of us grow up to be largely peaceful, as long as there is room for peace to evolve within and beyond war. There needs to be space enough to cultivate tranquility. We do that back-bending tending each and every day, redirecting our warrior skills toward tranquil ways. We must try to build peaceful shelters, instead of forts. We still need to give mutual support to succeed. We cannot do this alone; but we're already doing it together, just by being gracefully side by side.

To be in tranquility with war's practitioners, we need to have compassion enough for them to be truly present and know them. And who are war's practitioners? I'm one, and so are you. The seeds and roots of war are within every one of us.

War is as subtle as beauty. It has just as many layers as peace does, and many of those layers are miniature. If I make a comment to you that's aggressive, destructive and out of keeping with peaceful purpose, that's an act of war. At the core it's the spirit of our actions that makes war or peace. And it really doesn't matter how righteous our intentions are: peace, like love, isn't merely a feeling. It's a compassionate set of actions, taken skillfully enough to have positive consequences for all. So many causes with peaceful intent have fallen to war.

Even our homes, intended to be sanctuary, can be an act of war. In our own neighborhoods, **war is accidentally waged against the land and all species of its residents, through the weapon of excess.** Imbalance becomes violence. Excess becomes diminishment and war.

War can be found in the calmest places; yet tranquility can grow from the center of warlike ones. They're intertwined and co-exist together, just as we do.

We're still practitioners of our tiny daily wars as well as peace. As large as modern weapons have become, war is also very small and permeates as deeply as dust into water.

When war is so subtle and personal, we're most often at war in our daily lives with the ones with whom we're intimate. **All wars are family feuds, in the end.** Through conflict we learn about each other and are given the opportunity to become closer.

Our goal should not be to eliminate our conflicts, but to transform our methods of conflict resolution so that the damage we do is not so huge on the way to intimacy. Each footstep has to move to resolve conflicts rather than perpetuate them—a journey that strengthens us, not weakens us.

In order to move to this place of less destructive, more highly evolved conflict resolution, all we have to do is learn better expressions of our natural tendencies. We must find the courage to live with smaller weapons again, and recognize that we can't wait for others to be the first to reduce scale. We have to sense how larger weapons create larger enemies.

We also have to know that **we become like those we fight.**

Didn't many Native Americans become much more like the white invaders, by picking up those invaders' weapons to try to repel them? Didn't modern Americans become more like their 9/11 attackers, by responding to war with larger war? Might one of us have practiced war last night, by responding to an unkind comment with another?

Self-defense is as natural as conflict and competition. But we need to relearn the value of vulnerability. We need to recall what self-defense truly is, for it's as subtle, small and deep as war.

True self-defense is living in a compassionate way that doesn't create unnecessary conflict. It's caring for the earth. It's cultivating food, hauling water, treating illness—especially for those with whom we disagree. It's sheltering those around us who need it. It's selfless service. It's listening to others' legitimately different ways of feeling and being. It's honoring views we don't understand. It's sharing our abundance in a way that doesn't invite attack. It's recognizing that dominance doesn't bring security, but instead creates violent imbalance.

Self-defense is in recognizing, admitting and working to change our own role in unnecessary conflict. It's education—of ourselves at least as much as others. Self-defense is a practice of openness and trust—another shared creation that cannot be practiced alone. And our practice will always need to be practiced a bit better again tomorrow. It does become easier, though. Grace and tranquility become a relaxing meditation and a habit.

No matter the intrinsic nature of conflict, large wars need not always continue. As inevitable as these wars' beginnings seem to be, so is their end. **All warriors die.** Each new generation tears the old warmongers faces from the walls.

And what's inside the emptiness of each warmonger's eyes? Space enough for new peaceful leaders to grow—ones who may even be the offspring of the violent. There's always room for another generation of leaders who've learned from the mistakes of the past. The wise are always here among us; they'll become leaders if we learn to walk their paths with them. And the only way to do so is to be such leaders ourselves. After enough generations of leadership, graceful new instincts of tranquility will evolve.

As we honor and become new leaders, we'll get nostalgic at times for our previous flawed leaders. We'll wish for their resurrection, once their faults are too distant for clear memory.

The greatest leaders often remain unnoticed in the shadows

around us. For example, leaders of a remnant tribe in a land now called Canada are still open enough to share one last sacred shred of land with the descendents of their conquerors, still able to address them as friends.

That's master gardening. That's creating a habitat in which peace can thrive, through constant tending by example, even in the face of great loss and adversity.

Grace and tranquility must be practiced in small places, daily. So let's not think it in vain to declare tiny corners

of our homes to be international peace zones. This one in Mexico is parallel in a way to the Canadian one thousands of miles north.

In whatever land we find ourselves in, let's rest along its avenues and discover small tranquil places. Let's breathe quietly, for silence is tranquil, too. What's more peaceful than a silent mind?

We'll discover with true patience that what we would've waited for is already here. Tranquility is always flitting in on tiny insect wings, unnoticed unless we're still enough to see.

In the end, we're like any others straining imperfectly to express our serenity, with our grace and uniqueness found within imperfection itself. I may mean peace with my words, but if I paint them on your wall, you may not greet their presence with tranquility. **Only you can tell me if I've accidentally, unskillfully, intimately declared war with my words to you.** Only you can peacefully forgive me. It's within forgiveness that we find tranquility in our intimacy with war.

Governmedia

One element of tranquility is finding peace with government. But who and what truly govern us? Government is so much more subtle than just an administration or a stately set of buildings to house their pretenses of power. We're all governed by forces far deeper than democracy or dictatorship.

Beyond reach of legislation, we're governed within by our needs, beliefs, emotions and desires. Externally, we're governed by nature's ways and forces. **We're governed as much by greater mystery as by anything known.** In the face of that, humility, listening and respect for true greater governance are perfect, graceful steps toward tranquility. We're here in service to that governing universe, even as we're also an essential, beautiful piece of it, with our own evolving ways to contribute to the organic shifts of the natural order.

Within the reach of the little human structures we've created to manage ourselves, government—in its more traditional sense—has found its definition and reputation bent under the weight of misuse. It would seem at times that government is only a corrupt conspiracy to take our money, take over other lands and take power for a few at the expense of many. Too often that dark shadow of government is real, and at the expense of not just the human many, but also of the multitudes of other beings alongside us. **What a brilliant diversity of life there is here, governed by much deeper spirit than Congress!**

First and foremost, govern- ment is us—a portion of our soul, extended to visibility within the community. It's collectively here to serve our needs. This means serving the greater context of the earth that nurtures us—

including the other humans with whom we conflict. **The taxes we pay, the liberties we defend, are in truth loving acts to serve the generation we're raising to follow in our footsteps.** If we govern well, they'll follow by being a little more peaceful and loving than we've been.

In recent decades, much of what's labeled "progress" has been technological, although **new technology always breeds new bugs.** Much of what's technological has been given the blurry name of "the media." So, what of this evolving form of life and power we call the media?

This vague collective has begun to effectively govern individual perceptions, feelings, beliefs and resulting actions. The media's effects upon us in turn affect the rest of government. Eventually, all within this planet's holistic life are touched by the human media—even those species in fields, forests and seas who've never perceived its existence.

The media are a neutral conduit. Radio, television, the Internet: like painting, photography, language itself, they're vessels that hold and reflect our highest potential and our egregious flaws. When they illuminate life in a compassionate, truthful way, they're a beautiful miracle. But when they become a replacement for direct experience, they're illusion instead—and a dangerous, distorted one at that. The more they replace direct experience, the more

difficult it is for us to even recognize the distortion. We lose our grounded reference point for comparison.

Government and media and our own souls become beautiful with our best, and tainted by our worst. The governmedia become exactly what we are, and what we deserve them to be. So in order for the governmedia to evolve, we'll have to evolve inside. We'll have to make it a priority to bring beauty, compassion and tranquility forward together on a daily basis as we walk these paths. We'll have to refocus on the beautiful plants and creatures at our feet, and on gardening the greater life that supports us all. When we reflect these priorities insistently enough, our media and our government will reflect them as well, of their own peaceful accord.

The Beauty
of Doubt

In the soft reflection of spirit, we can see ourselves and the wind of richness in everything. There's clarity in the reflection at times, if we're present enough and still enough to be observant, and if the wind is calm enough that day to allow it. Yet even in the stillest dawn, the reflection of the heavens is often muted, translated. It's incomplete even in its perfect beauty. In that reflection we see our own incompleteness and perfect beauty.

It's easy to seek certainty, to desire exact knowledge of tomorrow and how the greater heavens work. There's no tranquility within that, though—it's an impossible demand that we reach such perfect understanding. Our most refined religious conceptions can never take us there, no matter how much comfort they provide.

injury with completeness? Only then can we move forward into letting go. There's no true healing method but embrace.

Many injuries leave permanent scars; some may be disfiguring. But **the presence or shape of our scars has no effect on deeper beauty or forgiveness.** Our scars themselves may come to seem beautiful when we integrate and accept them. Forgiveness returns us to this stable, tranquil equilibrium.

How are great acts of forgiveness possible? In part, by seeing the potential darkness within our own souls. Personal and global history shows how possible it is for each and every one of us, under unbearable pressure and pain, to climb that scale to unspeakable blind action. Thrown off-center in the fiercest of storms, we become distorted in the present tense and in our sense of our own history.

To be able to practice forgiveness well means knowing that the ones who've wounded us are kin. The hurtful and the wounded can easily trade places. We have to acknowledge our potential to injure each other and the earth.

Having compassion for this in ourselves allows us to deepen compassion for others and forgive them.

It may take a lifetime to integrate all we've suffered, and all the suffering we've caused. We may not even be finished when we go. Forgiveness can take generations. We may grow old long before admitting that what's bothered us about each other is what's bothered us about ourselves. We'll express outrage about the environment while driving our belching car. We'll speak of peace and plan for war. We'll curse China for crushing Tibet while forgetting Native America's similar plight. We'll speak of one all-encompassing spirit, and then start a war when another's conception of that spirit doesn't fit within our tiny view. **Little that appears black and white truly is.**

So let's **praise the bright and subtle shades of color that surround us.** Let's walk in the cathedral of autumn trees once more and practice letting go. Let our beliefs be leaves: our release of them will nurture the next return of spring. We will grow fresh beliefs when it's time.

If we keep walking with compassion, hand in hand, seeing clearly the wholeness in each other, both dark and light, we can release the latest cycle of injuries. We can be released in turn and come to rest. Just that knowledge alone soothes a wound just a little.

May Peace Prevail On Earth

Tranquility
in Patience

Millions of winters have stormed in and then receded. After all of the wisdom that's sprouted and faded again with the seasons, wars still rage, evolving as other life does. **New snows fall on our monuments to wishes that wars would cease.** Winter always returns, insistently.

Under these conditions, it's easy to fall into the delusion that peace has never visited this planet, and never will. But wait: again we're looking for a peace too large and constant to be real.

Even in the most persistent storms, others before us have managed to make tough times home. They created love there, and families and laughter. Surely they had tranquil times within the struggle. Much of the peaceful wisdom is ancient. Countless wise ones have walked before us. Many have met more difficult challenges than we have, despite access to less resources and riches. Many have done so with their souls at peace. The successful practice of tranquility is an art as ancient as humanity—perhaps as ancient as all life.

There are countless paths that lead to our serene evolution. But just as the available peace may not be a large one, the paths may be very small. They may not be doors of governmental relations. We may grow impatient with our supposed leaders, but we need not wait for them. **Doors to peace reach citizen to citizen, in the strangest and simplest places.**

Tranquility might be in a meal shared or a piece of music jointly listened to, a feeling understood. The truest peace negotiations are those born of love across any distance, and a curiosity of culture—an ability to see common connections within a celebration of differences. Kind communication with a stranger is a peace treaty that needs no negotiation. True peace is practiced, not negotiated. It is practiced with patience and persistence, which are elements of grace themselves.

Musicians, dancers and **artisans of all forms can be some of the greatest ambassadors of peace.**

So can athletes. And scientists. Doctors. Taxi drivers. Anyone whose interests and love transcend the empty stories of history that divide us is practicing peace. Anyone whose practice in the moment is sharing, not grasping.

That practice requires patient stillness as well as active accomplishment. So let's practice together in silence for a moment now.

Silence is just music waiting to happen. And it can happen anywhere. Music is an ever-present ambassador of peace, an endless offering of tranquility.

It is with sound as it is with the very fabric of the universe: most of it is open space. How much peaceful possibility that creates room for! What beautiful music fills it, if we choose! And what a beautiful quiet returns, the instant we cease our noise.

Another breath in, another breath out. There is time.

There's another reason to be still and silent: **it's often the quietest voice that speaks the clearest truth.** That voice may come from within us or beside us, but without our stillness and silence its wisdom may drown in the din. To just be silent while attentively listening is one of our greatest conflict resolution skills, whether the conflict is purely internal or consuming the world.

It takes patience to practice listening long enough to hear the smallest, quietest voices. It takes more patience to put the voices' wisdom into quiet practice. To be contemplative is emotionally risky, because it requires that we open ourselves to heightened sensitivities. We become vulnerable and release our defenses.

Still, within shared contemplative silence is deeper safety. It prevents us from practicing any form of war, here, now, for this moment. And as long as we're doing the work that heads toward peace, we can feel tranquil. We can make this hard time home. No need to sit and scan the horizon, waiting in vain for rescue. We can rescue ourselves with simple silence.

Those who love the mystery of questions have a far easier time embracing grace and practicing tranquility than those who demand definitive answers. The quietest voice we hear in our most meditative state may ask questions rather than answer them. They may just be wiser questions.

We will never run out of questions, because the wider we open ourselves through stillness, the wider the mystery we see. **Our tranquility is in falling in love with the greater unknown, in seeing its beauty without a need to understand.** We are not seeking anything except to be with it.

Fishermen know a great deal about this state of contemplative presence—at least, fishermen who sense that fishing, not catching fish, is the essence of the experience. They of all people know patience. A bite on the line would be nice, and could even be dinner.

But just to be with the river! To be out, deeply with the water and the creatures who swim it! What a communion at streamside, with the air and the noise of the rapids, with the birds nestled in the trees! A fish is like an answer. A fish is not necessary to have a peaceful day.

If we have patience and presence, soon enough we notice the beauty surrounding us more than our questions. **Questions may become forgotten or irrelevant, compared to the elegance of the earth underfoot.** Like fishermen, we may soon be so absorbed in the beauty of the water that time and fish disappear from mind.

Beauty will wait for us to become this present, for as long as it takes. Our lives may be rapid, yet beauty can be glacially slow. Beauty was here long before we came, and will be here long after we've rejoined the dust. **Beauty is not in a hurry.** Beauty's more patient than a fisherman. Beauty doesn't need to change. Beauty itself is peace.

Given a context of acceptance in which to grow, beauty changes anyway. It evolves, too. Eventually the beauty of water smoothes

the stone, the seemingly impenetrable splits into openness and growth makes its way through to the light. *Patience was worth it*, the quietest tranquil voice says then.

Imagination as Foundation

Along paths of grace, I hear wise voices whisper of the importance of keeping two grounded feet. But **what are wings for, if not to use them?** Just stay cognizant of the shifting wind. Then fly with abandon! Once we reach the great heights, soaring often takes less effort than standing. The muscular wind will carry us. It knows how.

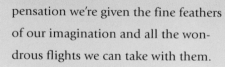

We may not have been given physical wings, but in compensation we're given the fine feathers of our imagination and all the wondrous flights we can take with them.

Imagination is essential for far more than dreams. It's the skill that allows us to see what's real through another's eyes—one of the most productive actions we can take if we want to gracefully evolve into tranquility. **Imagination is the foundation of compassion.**

93

Imagination is also practical: **common vision and conventional wisdom don't solve our deepest, most persistent problems.** Otherwise, those troubles wouldn't remain. Imaginative visions merge with conscious action to provide new insight and solutions. Those visions can be as small as deciding where to place our feet next, given our effect on all those underfoot. Imagination can be as small as any of the tiny beings around us, and still be as essential as those lives.

Like any skill, imagination expands with daily use. Flights of childhood fancy form the foundation of creative adults. Imaginative adults are then able to envision lives and contexts beyond the ordinary, and bring them into being. Without imagination, dull stasis would rule. We'd see every scene too literally and fail to leave room for imagination's flights.

No matter how effective and intense our imagination may be, it's hard to conjure a vision as creative as what's real.

What's vital is that our own paths and the contexts that open around them are equally unexpected. All paths and contexts are filled with possibility beyond belief, wilder than imagination. True possibility may first seem too strange to be real, but once we become accustomed to tranquility, to lasting love, to other strange beauty, it simply becomes normal and natural. That, too, is natural and comforting.

Trusting in that eventual comfort is of great use in daring to imagine what beautiful visions can be turned into reality. **Sometimes we must fly alone, away from the familiar, to find peace.** We must fly into open and unprotected air. Dare to imagine that cold edge and the thrill of near weightlessness.

Flying from the familiar often doesn't feel graceful in the short run. That cold edge, that thrill: they're anything but tranquil at first. Still, the stifling stasis of the overly familiar—where we let our imaginative visions go, in favor of the mundane and barely acceptable—is lethal to tranquility over time. Better to risk beauty and imagination, chancing that it will fail us, than to marry the certainty of failing ourselves and each other.

We can imagine—and truly find—grace and tranquility almost anywhere. Peace is in being in service to the whole, until it's our turn to leave—to feel the lightness of the soaring bird at last, free to migrate with loved ones to the next place we imagine home to be. **Even seemingly weightless freedom is a long perilous journey, though.** Tranquility is a flight that requires aligning with the differing rhythms of so many others. It's in daring the long journey anyway, when instinct calls for it to be made—no matter the outcome.

There are moments in our lives—sometimes even whole lives—in which **grace is in celebrating others' flight, though we ourselves are grounded.**

Tranquility via observation can be a difficult attainment when we're confronted with an impossible urge to soar. But that's only our painful ego, wishing to be all things—imagining it as a need.

There's often tranquility in not having to fly. There's relief in the beauty of just watching. There's serenity in observing what we do not need to do. Imagine, for a moment, all the jobs that others did today, that we will never have to do. Our gratitude for their efforts needs to be far more than imagination. Our gratitude is our grace and tranquility.

Tranquility is also in doing our best to land softly when the flight of our life is done. Whatever light and feathery memories we may leave behind, tranquility is in knowing that we've done our best and can rest, nestled in the fading colors of another passing season. When we imagine that peaceful rest, we move closer to bringing it into being.

Aligning with Purpose

No stone is extraneous. Each one has purpose and beauty. Each plays its perfect part in making the ground under our feet solid. (Who could keep grounded feet without the ground?)

There was also no such thing as a weed until we came along to name it—to project emptiness and uselessness upon a living being that had a perfectly natural place.

We're not extraneous either, no matter how much illusions conspire sometimes to make us feel that way—for waste is a purely human concept.

In the natural system, waste does not exist. One kind of life is food for the next. What one creature discards or excretes, in some way always feeds the whole. In our divergence, **we've created not only waste, but the very idea of it.**

Knowing that waste is illusory, we can have more confidence in taking our places here.

If purpose calls you to be the single odd blade of grass in a field of flowers, so be it. **You are not a so-called "weed." Flowers are not more valid than grass or thorns.**

If it is your fate to bloom, you must dare to bloom to your fullest, even if the incongruous singularity of your beauty seems to leave you out of place and vulnerable. **To not bloom when it's possible would be the closest to waste that there is.**

Whatever our purpose in the greater weave, centering in grace and tranquility means finding and accepting that purpose. What have we really come here to do?

Our purpose may be beautifully small. In the natural world, purpose is very simple. The purpose of these water drops is simply to nurture. And they don't need to nurture the whole earth to fulfill their purpose. Each drop only has to nurture one tiny piece of soil for one moment in order for its purpose to be fulfilled. There's no large burden for any one drop to carry. Together, they gather strength. It's the same for us and our collective purpose.

Our collective purpose may be to simply stand here and bloom together. That purpose is perfectly in keeping with the evolution of nature—our nature. It doesn't have to be more complicated than that.

Unfortunately, we've cluttered purpose with the concept of work, tragically separating the two. For so many, work feels like chains and fences rather than the brightness that shines through them.

Part of the tragedy is how closely associated work, suffering, and money have become. It distracts from the deeper, purer truth: **Work is about service; and service is about joy.** It's about contribution to the greater cause of life—a cause in which our needs as individuals are best served by placing our focus on the greater good. Good work is transparent. We can see through it to its greater purpose, to its role in making this planet a better place to live. This alignment of work and purpose is what allows us to greet our daily tasks with grace and tranquility.

Ideally, our work and purpose merge so smoothly that retirement becomes meaningless—for ceasing to work then means ceasing to live.

Our purpose may be medicine or housekeeping, parenting or sculpting or politics. It may be growing food for others or shaping vessels for water. It may be celebrated or ignored, joyful or tedious. That doesn't matter. If it contributes to the joy of greater service, it's valuable.

If fully merging work and purpose proves elusive or transient, **our modest purpose can be to bring vibrancy into whatever dull task is at hand.** The care, the compassion, the joy and pride we bring to our tasks every day have a vast effect on drawing the richness out of emptiness—not only for ourselves but for those around us.

How many retail clerks have truly changed your day with a simple smile or a radiant way? Theirs is the essence of effective purpose, and its ability to beautifully change the world is immense. It's the equal of bird song, also sung while finding the means for survival—to live long enough to contribute another generation of song.

Purpose doesn't have to mean doing more than we already are, either. Doing less often allows us the space to do what we do effectively, joyfully, mindfully.

Neither does purpose remain fixed. From moment to moment, year to year, our purpose will shift. From taking the trash out to caretaking the elderly, from literature to laundry, there are many aspects to purpose.

The humbling aspects of purpose teach a strong lesson: **the by-products of our work are just as important as the work we intend to do.** Both exist. Both are therefore equal. To the earth, there is no difference between our trash and our treasure, our intended creations and the actual result. The building we build in which to do our work has as much effect as what we do inside. Our accidents equal our intentions.

When we really open our minds to this equality, the illusion disappears that we have no effect upon the world. Every glance, every breath has an effect—and we have a responsibility for them. Making a meaningless motion is impossible.

Equality within purpose allows us to stand with the most majestic trees and be of equal stature. When we're truly grounded in purpose and its majesty, we can stand at the foot of a stunning, sacred mountain and humbly say yes, we belong here, we're worthy, we're home. In our own way, we're as beautiful, rich and vital. We must own our vital beauty without ego, for equality will also remind us that the earthworm underfoot also has a matching majesty.

Our purpose and place may shift in an instant.
Equality of majesty gives every life equal chance to be absorbed back into earth's continuance—not as waste, but as food. It could happen at any moment. The trees above, for instance, were as majestic and purposeful as any, standing in perfect service to the beautiful slopes of Mt. St. Helens when the mountain exploded. Now they are in perfect service to the new form of the area, the regeneration of life that is daring to take place, with imagination and persistence. Beauty never left and again dares to show its shy face. Purpose remains unscathed.

The ease with which our personal form can disappear is a fine reminder of how quickly our small essential purpose can shift, at the whim of a mountain or far smaller forces.

In the end, fulfilling purpose is not dependent upon how well we feed ourselves. It's more dependent upon how well we feed others around us, from blade of grass to greater spirit, from partner in intimacy to opponent in war. **If we're conscious enough to be of essential service, our species will thrive, in direct reflection of that which thrives around us.** All will be at peace within purpose and the joy of service.

The Banks of Clear Streams

Seeing iconic religious statues for sale, I laugh. **Do even saints have their price?** How do we find tranquility with money? For most of us, it isn't an easy peace.

Finding tranquility with money parallels finding it with conflict in intimacy. We have to learn to be at peace with its presence, rather than seeking its absence. No matter any saintly ideals about casting money aside, the cost of necessities means we all wear price tags. Money's rooted so deeply into the living weave that freedom from it is unrealistic—and if peace needs to be anything, it needs to be realistic.

It's an easy illusion that the way to be at peace with money is to have a lot of it. That narrow form of abundance does ease some burdens, but it also creates burdens of its own. Increased financial resources only increase happiness at low levels of poverty. Above that, money's positive contributions are balanced by the headaches of managing it, the addictive lure of seeking more of it, the complications of possessions acquired by using it, the fear of losing it, the guilt at having it, the free time lost from simpler and deeper forms of happiness because of it, and so on.

The earthly pool of money is much like a vast pool of water. We need a certain intake from it for our lives to be nourished and healthy. Too much of it, though, and it becomes dangerous. Drowning is one outcome from excessive income. Stashing a vast quantity of money is unnecessary anyway, if the streams around us are kept running clear and accessible to all.

Money stagnates as much as water does if it's dammed and hoarded. Then it can't be tasted by those who need it; it won't run free to nourish the living landscape. It becomes easily tainted—polluted the same as a sea. It needs to keep flowing from hand to hand in a shared, generous way to keep running clear.

Unlike a pool of water, money is our own creation. It's directly reflective of our souls, and the issues it causes are nothing but issues of our own invention.

Is it any wonder that money has so much power over us, when we're the parent of it? **Money is the difficult child we love yet fault because it's too much like us.** We may fight money bitterly every day—and still miss it terribly when it's gone.

So money is family, and we're intimate with it—just as intimate as we are with deeper spirit—and there's no clear border between spirit and money. That's evolution: money's found a way to come to life as a species, and carved out a niche within the food chain. It can be as evil or pure as the one who directs its flow. So being in tranquility with money means being at peace with our ability to direct it to where the growth needs it.

Being in tranquility with money is just a small part of recognizing and being at peace with the natural state of abundance around us, as we walk alongside the banks—not only the banks of money, but the banks of clear streams of water, air, spirit, purpose, community. **Abundance takes endless forms in this lifelong walk, merely waiting to be recognized.**

Time's Laughter

Listen! Can you hear time laughing? Time is a living cousin too. Time, who holds all abundance in hand. Time, who cradles us far beyond our birth and death. **Time is abundance itself.**

We might as well laugh with time while it still grants us life. That way, we can let go of so many of the fears that have tightly bound us. They're small compared to the earth around us, and they'll be over soon enough. We can release their weight and let go into the discovery that life doesn't have to be held so heavily, even at its worst. One of the greatest philosophical questions is still this: So what? If we can keep a true enough sense of our essential small place, we can ask that question easily. And then we can laugh and laugh at how seriously we used to take things.

Do you mind for a moment if I talk to you more personally about time? My father called just after I first wrote those last lines. He was dealing then with the isolation of aging, the difficulty of watching lifelong friends return to the earth. Time seemed to be laughing at him, not with him. (Time only sighs for him now. He's ash at sea.)

He called that day to ask for help in finding a certain book of humor, to share with the wife of a friend now back in the soil. The book was to remind her of the laughter the three shared. "The most important task is to participate with joy in the sorrows of the world," he quoted, attributing the words to Buddha.

His call reminded me of when I was stricken with cancer in my early thirties. After two surgeries, I'd moved on to chemotherapy and shared a room with many other cancer patients who also had plenty of free time to sit and ponder, as the life-saving poison was dripped into our veins. Since cancer is an equal-opportunity employer, it was a room full of diverse humanity—not only in age,

ethnicity, gender and other easy measures, but also in outlook and attitude. I met a dying teenage girl who was far happier and more full of laughter—different concepts—than the sixty-year-old man beside me who'd already had a good life and still had a high chance of survival. There was no discernable connection in that room between prognosis and disposition—though as I came to learn later, the happier are a little more likely to heal.

When time is so measurably precious, it's more important than ever to laugh *now*. There are no opportunities to waste. When we're dying or in danger of it—and who isn't?—enjoying that perfect

strawberry or hot bath or deep laugh doesn't become trivial; it becomes more important and enjoyable than ever.

One of the surest ways to tranquility is to realize we're all dying from our day of birth. The more deeply we feel this, the more precious our days become. We know: no moment is extraneous. There is no waste.

This moment is no less capable of holding richness than any other moment, either. Time is equally weighted. And this moment deserves deep gratitude for its existence. Gratitude, again the shortest path to experiencing grace and tranquility.

There's no clear difference between living and dying. We're all constantly doing both, and we have been since the dawn of the universe. We might as well keep doing it with joy and a sense of humor.

Humor is both wisdom and a survival tactic—and not merely the province of humans. How much happier and more harmonious we'd be if we practiced the innate wisdom of humor more skillfully in our daily conflicts!

Listen again: we can not only hear time and its laughter, we can *feel* time blowing through everything, another insistent living wind. Time has such pure force. It's invisible, and its true nature is unfathomable—yet it's so powerful and indisputable. Time has mass, as surely as the largest boulder or galaxy.

Time is even more massive than the galaxies combined; for it changes the form of all of them at once. Is time the communication of spirit, speaking to us with tiny bits of some larger language that we'll never have the sense or senses to understand? Time *is* a language of some ethereal form, and like spoken language it begins to settle into our physical body over time and sculpt it. Is time simply the artistry of God?

Time laughs with joy at our little questions.

Becoming the Harvest

The ideal end result of farming is to make all the fruits of growth disappear. All the tilling, planting, watering, weeding and other nurturing that brings a crop to fruition is done in service to it being picked and consumed. The harvest is the celebrated moment at which disappearance begins.

The process is similar to what we bring to fruition with our lives. We feed the ones around us with our gifts and then disappear. Our disappearance is essential, if others are to grow. If the beauty our lives created was permanent, the world would fill up with it. It would become harder and harder for new souls to find a place for their own beauty. New individuals would become less and less useful. Beauty, purpose, life itself: they need to fade to be refreshed. So it's a blessing that no matter how vibrant the colors we bring to the world, eventually they fade and peel and vanish. **Fading and disappearance are a part of beauty, rather than a diminishment of it.**

One universal law of beauty seems to be that the shorter a bloom is visible, the more brilliantly beautiful it is. Brief blooms cannot take the chance that their beauty will not be enough to attract the ones they need to be touched by, to carry the cycle of beauty on.

This may be the natural function of our own brevity here: to make sure we're beautiful enough. The more acutely aware of our brevity we are, the more insistent we become about bringing forth all our beauty. Living fully is the path that precludes regret—the path of maximum giving to others' growth, before the beauty of our bloom fades to silhouette.

The faded form of all we bring into being is as much our creation as what we initially grow and give. Ideally, if we're looking deeply enough into what we create, we'll envision its graceful fading as skillfully as its first form. We'll envision our creations in several generations' time. Yet that's often beyond us. Bringing life and beauty into being remains a partnership between our vision and larger spirit.

How we perceive rust may well predict how we feel about ourselves as we look in the mirror in old age.

Do we see "Beautiful British Columbia" in contrast to the rust, or is the rust beautiful itself? Is it alive? And did we take generations of rust into account in our designs?

Can we see our wrinkles and gray as an accomplishment? Can we feel our lingering gifts and memories as a beautiful, sufficient harvest? Can we be tranquil sitting in a street-side chair as young, loving couples appear like letters from our younger selves? Can we be at peace with postcards from places we can no longer visit? Can we relax into our elderly beauty without a demand for changeless eternity?

There's tranquility inside the embrace of silhouettes and memories, even though there's pain, too. There is grace.

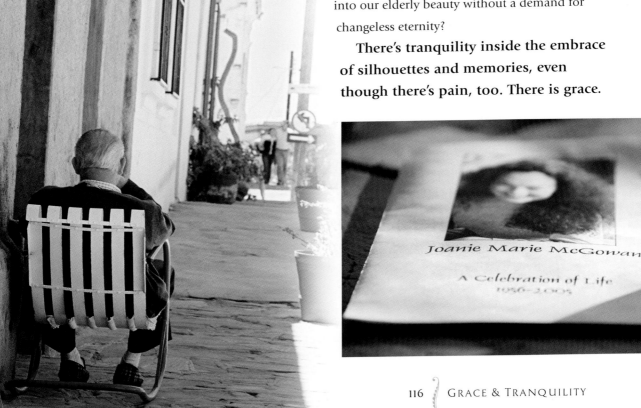

BEAUTIFUL
KKR·608
BRITISH   COLUMBIA

Joanie Marie McGowan

A Celebration of Life
1936–2005

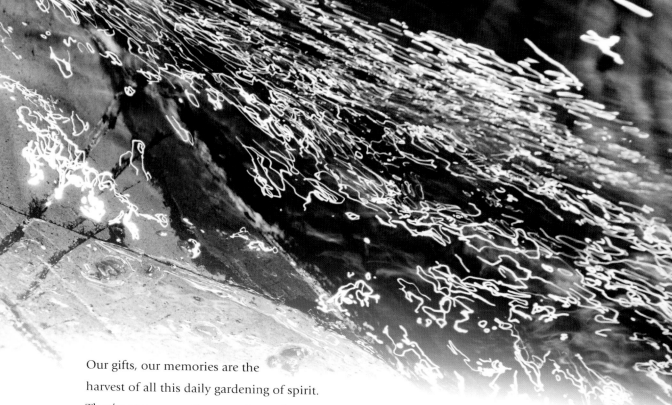

Our gifts, our memories are the
harvest of all this daily gardening of spirit.
They're one reason that even in a culture obsessed with the
surface beauties of youth, the old are more likely to be happy than
the young.

We're regal in silhouette. Knowing that is part of the process of
seeing beauty in everything—which is the process of living in tranquility's light. So often silhouettes clarify form. They reduce com-
plication to essential shapes.

Our task in seeing silhouettes, especially of people, is to look
deeply and skillfully enough to see which elements are truly essential. What did they bring when they were here? What tracers of brilliant light did they leave to linger with us?

We all leave tracers, as sunlight does on a river.

The light of our lives subtly shines and reflects. The tracers we
leave may be so brief and in such constant motion that they're difficult to clearly see with the naked eye. Yet they are brilliant. All we
become and affect is essential to those who come before and after

us. From some perspective apart from our limited notions of time, every detail of history is permanently carved into the universe. We are an element of that history. The equality of majesty says our history is carved as sharply as anyone else's.

The practice of seeing others' silhouettes and tracers, and of recognizing our own, is vital to our daily peace. It brings honor and respect for the role of all living beings, including ourselves. It illuminates the value of all creatures in the past, present and future. The more we open our vision to see the subtle tracers of lives, the more brilliant the world we see— and even then, we can only glimpse bits of it. Our senses are so limited, our touches so incomplete even in their perfection. We can look deeply into each other's eyes and listen to every nuance of expression, and inevitably we'll still only know the slightest amount of all that each of us feels and dreams and is.

We'll never cultivate personal immortality in the way our dreams imagine, but since energy and spirit are ceaseless, there is no death beyond our own, merely new space left for new life to fill. **Continuance of life and its harvest is not only achievable, it's inevitable.**

Within the impermanence of our shifting forms is a larger permanence—just another return to where the truth always leads: to the richness inside the emptiness. It returns to the grace and tranquility always resting at the core.

The living and dead support each other in cycles of perfect continuance. As a leaf shifts from green to gray to gone, its nutrients return to the soil right there to feed the very bush it came from and all the life to which that plant is linked. It's nature's efficient truth again: none of us are lost. None of us will ever be wasted.

No matter if we're aging and if it first seems our footprints quickly fade from the surface. **How incredibly powerful we are, to contain history and trigger the future!** It's an amazing bounty, this harvest we are—bound to inspire silent awe when we discover its vastness inside us.

That silence of awe: we'll each carry it with us when our voices have spoken all they've come here to say, and relax at last into rest. It's a profound, peaceful silence—one without regret, one that needs no effort to be sustained.

The vastness of the harvest is in every small place. Let's abandon all sense of time and scale. They're mostly creations of our limited perception, anyway. It's normal that trees appear bigger than the mountains and the sun. Who's to say they aren't, when every tiny vista opens up into enough beauty to swallow it all? **This open space beside us and within us: we'll disappear inside it forever but we'll never be lost.**

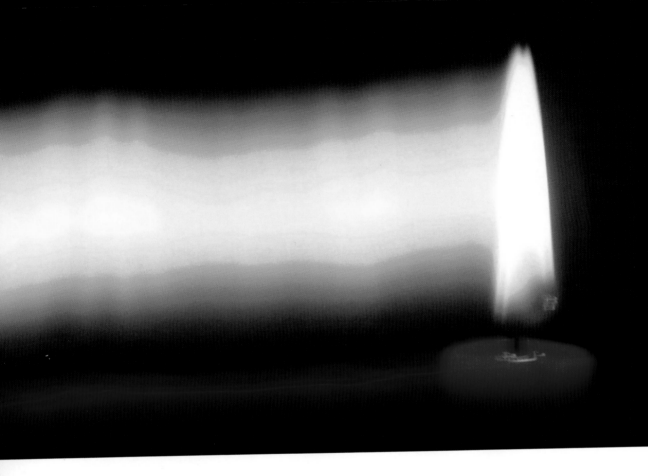

Intimate with Integrity

As we move through the open space that cradles everything, acting with integrity is essential to keeping our lives centered in serenity. Integrity's light illuminates our path, even though it flickers and dances and sometimes dims. With every motion in every storm, we have to shelter and shape our integrity to keep it from being extinguished.

Our personal integrity evolves into being along with us. It's always fragile and endangered, as we are. It can vanish in an instant. Our integrity's individual life can also be magnificent, unexpected, and in conflict with others. Its complexities can be mystifying. **Integrity can be a source of wonder as deep as any surrounding beauty.**

Integrity is a form of service and an alignment with purpose—not only honoring our own purpose in every moment and action, but the purpose of others around us, within our shared cause of nurturing the sacred greater life. Integrity means gathering our strength in a way that doesn't diminish others. Integrity means action without deception. Integrity treats every daily interaction as one with beloved close family. Integrity demands constant compassion: truth spoken kindly, hands held without falsity. It means conflict resolution that honors the interests of the ones with whom we conflict. It means owning our doubt and being willing to stand corrected. **Integrity has as many meanings as there are moments and people.** Becoming intimate with it means sensitivity to its context and ever-shifting form.

Whatever our current personal meaning for it, nothing is more vital than integrity in walking a tranquil path. Integrity is a clear avenue to serenity in memory, as we later take measure of our lives.

Transition's
Ceaseless Seas

124

If we look deeply enough as we travel, we'll see dimensions of beauty we never knew existed, and forms of tranquility imagination couldn't conjure.

These aspects of tranquility may seem separate from us at first, but as change washes over us and through us, it merges with us. **Transition is what creates us, and there is no more beautiful sight.**

As days themselves transition, we can share a sunrise and a sunset—a day's beginning and ending—from the same place. Can we be sure which is which? Can we really mark any moment at which days begin and end, knowing the cycle repeats and refreshes? Isn't dissecting the day's structure just a distraction from our real purpose here, of witnessing

and being the depth of the earth's beauty? **If we don't take the time to witness and be this beauty, who will?** If we don't take the opportunity to be tranquil, why not? It's up to us to experience this sacred richness, and by doing so mark it indelibly into the continuance of spirit.

Our eyes are naturally drawn to motion, which is transition. We're always watching change, and there's nothing more important than to pause to look a little more deeply into it. **There's no richer travel in this available breath than to simply pause and see.**

We're traveling even as we pause, across the arcs of orbits and time. Let those arcs do our work for this moment—this precious moment of vision. Let backward and forward lose their meaning as beginnings and endings do, as we step off the treadmill of time.

Walking
Softly Beyond

We'll never be alone in taking tranquil steps, or basking in the light of grace—not even when the shadows of our days grow long and the sun feels faint and chill.

Even if we look and think we see no one, others' continuance is always with us. The lands we walk have been sculpted by all who came before us. There's an entire archaeology of footsteps below where our feet are this very instant, reaching back to a time when this language we speak was not yet imagined. All the history that's happened here—all the feelings, thoughts and experiences of others—are still coded in the soil and air. Long ages of future experiences are also coded there, yet to reveal themselves.

The rich archaeology of spirit and experience has far more living dimensions than the human way of being. Those with wings have previously crossed this air, especially in the time before walls. Creatures of countless forms both within and above ground have also left their imprint here; their spirit marks territory across geologic ages. Other living forms of spirit be-

yond our knowing surely inform this land's abundance as well, in ways our limitations will never allow us to comprehend. **It's good for us to look at what's before us and not know what it is: that nurtures our humility in the face of greater mystery.**

Walk Softly
On The
Earth

Given the abundant presence of life beyond perception, we must walk softly as we go, even if it is on hard bricks. That's essential, not only for the life we fail to sense, but also for our own lives. **Conservation is not merely an altruistic act: it's the one thing certain to directly feed us the most.** Nurturing the earth nurtures us.

These shifting sands we walk are not truly shoreline or sideline. They're as central as any place within transition's ceaseless seas. Our footsteps have irrevocably moved sand grains, and their future movement is forever altered as a result. **Small changes and waves propagate; any one of our single footsteps may alter the future in large ways we may never know.** However imperceptible, we leave our mark.

Our ancestors used quills to make their mark on history more visible to others. Their feathers and ink left reminders of their presence—not so different from the birds who leave feathers, reminding us of their place in this journey's history.

Individual drops of water gather strength upon those feathered inscriptions, each with enough richness and space within to contain entire small worlds of grace and tranquility. All we have to do is keep moving slowly enough and looking closely enough to notice.

We must keep looking above and within. **We must look deeply enough to see not just the flags of celebration and prayer, but the prayers themselves and their results.** Then we can feel all the layers of spirit left here by those who've walked before us. We can sense the tiny creatures in this air now, too small to draw our eyes. We can bring into our vision the immense number of others yet waiting to breathe, their future dependent on how we care for this air, on whether we imbue it with peace and insight or pessimism and destruction. We need to look deeply enough into this sky to see the galaxies there beyond imagining, their beauty and light too distant and massive to fathom. We must fully feel how lucky we are to receive the starlight after its lengthy journey to us. We must never lose sight of gratitude for inheriting the vast fortune of existence.

Constant gratitude is the essence of grace and tranquility. It's as subtle and faint as galactic light itself, and as omnipotent. If we can keep its light present in our awareness in even the darkest times, we will have reached true equanimity, and there will be no more work for us to do.

No more, that is, except to pass along that light and tranquility to all near enough to touch, so they can be next to receive it, to gather strength by adding to it and to keep it by opening up to let it go. That is our journey along these paths, our next step together toward home.

Meditation and Conversation:
A Guide to Further Inquiry

Every good book raises at least as many questions as it answers. Here are a few questions inspired by this book's dance with grace and tranquility, as a guide for further exploration beyond the bounds of these pages. The questions connect to the observations of each book section. More importantly, they connect to our daily motions through the world, and our common search for peace.

Awakening

What does it mean to you, to be awake?

Why is peace necessarily intricate and delicate?

With what conception of peace did you begin this book? Has it changed? If so, how?

The Pace of Peace

Why is wealth found more in giving than receiving?

What have you recently received by giving?

Why is peace best found at a patient pace?

A Small Peaceful Presence

Why is peace neither massive nor permanent?

Where do you spend the most time, daily? In what ways are you or are you not tranquil there?

What is the most chaotic place that you regularly experience? What small elements of tranquility reside there? How can those elements be expanded?

Inside the Living Storm

What does it mean in your own life that "peace is too important to be left just for peaceful moments"?

Do you fight against weather or other unchangeable conditions in your life? How can you better align with weather's ways and wisdom?

What are the healthy limits of accepting turmoil?

Gathering Strength

In what way does your own small strength serve the larger world?

When have you grown simply by firmly standing still? What was the growth?

What does it mean that "tranquility has hard points and sharp edges"?

Spaciousness (the Key)

What's the difference between emptiness and spaciousness?

In what ways do you currently feel empty inside? In what ways, spacious?

When you look within that current emptiness, what richness is contained there?

Into the Endless Richness

What tranquility, beauty and grace do you see in the scene around you at this moment?

What does it mean to you, to follow the path of your next single step?

A Peace of Abundance

What does abundance mean to you? What does it include?

What seeds are you planting and tending in your current daily life? What's growing unexpectedly? Is the unexpected also a part of your abundance?

Why is water central to every form of abundance?

A Gardener's Tranquility

Who and what are you currently shaping? How are they shaping you in return?

At this point in your life, in what ways do you feel you are blossoming? Do you have compassion for yourself in those areas where blossoming is difficult?

Family Letters

Do you trust the ones closest to you? Why or why not? In what ways?

Do you trust the earth, the soil, the air? What does trusting the earth mean?

What does the path of your personal life say to your family? What will your actions today communicate to them?

At Peace with Intimacy

What does it mean that "intimacy is truth"? How are honesty and intimacy related?

Why is intimacy inherently difficult as well as beautiful?

What are you intimate with, besides a romantic partner?

Intimate with War

Can tranquility be found within war? If so, how and where? If not, why not?

In what small daily ways are you at war, and with whom or what? Can you make peace?

Why do we resemble those we fight? Why do we fight those we resemble?

Governmedia

Besides our elected leaders, who and what are you governed by? In what ways?

How do the media shape the governance you practice over your own life?

How do government and media reflect who you are, personally?

The Beauty of Doubt

How does doubt allow us to have new perceptions?

At what points has doubt opened you to unexpected possibilities?

Can faith and doubt co-exist peacefully inside a person? Do they, in you?

Letting Wounds Go

Where in the elements of nature around you do you see examples of the essential nature of letting go? How does it parallel your own need for letting go?

Why, emotionally, is it necessary to embrace wounds fully before releasing them? How does the embrace create the release?

How does compassion lead to forgiveness?

Tranquility in Patience

How is tranquility a practice like yoga or meditation? How does it differ?

How does your patience serve your personal tranquility, and that of others beside you?

Why is learning to love mystery and the unknown an essential skill within the practice of tranquility?

Imagination as Foundation

Why is imagination necessary for understanding and compassion?

In what times of your life has your ability to imagine helped bring you closer to others?

What does it mean that "Imagination is practical"? How has it been so in your life?

Aligning with Purpose

What is your purpose? What do you contribute, and what more would you like to?

Who does your daily work serve? Is it aligned with your purpose? How and how not? How can you better align your love and work?

When you pass on, what do you feel you will need to have contributed or experienced in order to be at peace?

The Banks of Clear Streams

How does money disturb or create tranquility in your life?

Describe any differences there may be, in your view, between true abundance and monetary wealth. How are the two in harmony, and how in conflict?

Without needing more than you currently have, how can your relationship with money become more tranquil?

Time's Laughter

When time is abundant for you, what do you fill it with? Do you make tranquil choices?

How does the impermanence of life make it sweeter and easier?

What purpose does humor serve for you? How can you naturally bring it more into your daily environment?

Becoming the Harvest

What do you appreciate about aging?

Does the brevity of life increase its preciousness?

What forms of beauty do you see in the elderly in your life?

Intimate with Integrity

What does keeping integrity mean to you in your current personal life?

In what ways are you keeping and failing it? How can you deepen it?

Transition's Ceaseless Seas

In what ways are you presently in transition? How can you best bring forth the graceful and tranquil from within the transition?

How can slowing down in small ways assist you in creating larger positive transition?

Are you daily taking time to just be with beauty and stillness? How can you better integrate beauty and stillness into your daily routines?

Walking Softly Beyond

What direct evidence of previous generations and cultures do you see and feel in your daily life? How does it contribute to your own life?

What greater mystery do you see that intrigues you? How does not always knowing or understanding enrich your life?

Does gratitude inform your daily acts and feelings? What are you grateful for at this very moment?

ABOUT THE AUTHOR

PHOTO: TINA BOLLING

Eric Alan divides his time between Cottage Grove and Ashland, Oregon, while also exploring wild and civilized places beyond. As well as being an author, he is a photographer, lyricist, radio broadcaster and workshop leader. His previous book, *Wild Grace: Nature as a Spiritual Path*, has inspired workshops on the re-integration of nature into daily life, a regular column reaching several eastern states, and multi-media event collaborations with nationally recognized musicians. *Grace and Tranquility* is a companion book to a music CD of the same name, merging his words with the music of the band Gypsy Soul. He can be reached at eric@wildgrace.org.

For more information, visit www.wildgrace.org or www.whitecloudpress.com.